Mastering Security:

A Comprehensive Guide to

Safeguarding Your Organisation

INDEX of Content

Page	Description
2 - 5	Foreword by Bob Marshall
6	**Introduction**
8	**Chapter 1 Comprehensive Security Footprint Analysis**
9	Financial Security
16	Information Security
23	Human Security
30	Technical Security
35	Physical Security
40	**Chapter 2 Adaptive Security Environment Management**
41	Covert Security
45	Training and Development
58	Contingency Planning
63	Command and Control
67	Virtual Security Footprint in a Business Security Environment
72	**Conclusion - Building a Resilient and Secure Organisation**
74	**About the Author**

Foreword by Bob Marshall

Drawing upon over four decades of experience in the security sector, my journey began as a police officer in one of the most challenging regions of the UK. During this formative period, I encountered a wide array of security threats, from street-level crimes to sophisticated organised crime networks.

 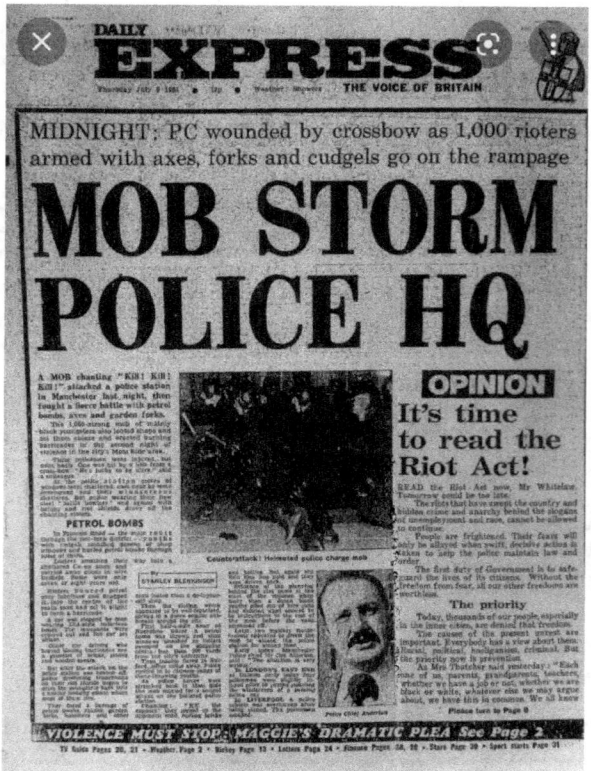

Moss Side Police Station on the morning of 9th July 1981 and Daily Express front page, the day after the riots in Manchester

These early experiences were instrumental in shaping my understanding of security's complexities and nuances, underscoring the need for a blend of strategic insight and tactical execution to achieve effective protection.

Over the years, I have been privileged to operate in some of the world's most dynamic and often high-risk environments. From conflict zones in Ukraine to burgeoning markets in the UAE, from the congested ports of Nigeria to the sophisticated urban centres of the USA, France, and Germany—each setting has broadened my understanding of security's multifaceted nature.

My career has taken me across Europe, the Middle East, Africa, and North America, and I have gained valuable insights working in countries such as Dubai, Iran, Qatar, Saudi Arabia, Cyprus, Albania, Denmark, Ireland, the Netherlands, Portugal, Slovakia, and Spain.

Every region I've worked in has presented its own unique set of challenges, ranging from geopolitical tensions and varying regulatory landscapes to cultural differences. Successfully navigating these diverse conditions has sharpened my ability to adapt and effectively apply my security expertise, establishing me as a trusted advisor to organisations of all sizes.

A group of Ukrainian soldiers leaving Lviv for the front-line April 2024, photographed with the author Bob Marshall

My experience spans a wide range of industries, each with its own distinct security needs and challenges. I have worked in pharmaceutical distribution and retail, which is heavily regulated and faces threats like theft and counterfeiting. I've dealt with the complexities of the transport and logistics sectors, where cargo security, route planning, and supply chain integrity are critical. In property management and warehousing, I have developed strategies to safeguard valuable assets through robust physical and operational security measures.

This diverse background has enabled me to cultivate a holistic approach to security consulting, ensuring that an organisation's security posture is both strong and adaptable to an ever-evolving threat landscape.

This book is a distillation of the knowledge and insights I have acquired over forty years into a practical, actionable guide. It is designed to help you conduct a thorough security analysis and develop a comprehensive security strategy tailored specifically to your organisation's needs. Whether you are seeking to enhance your current security measures or to build a new strategy from scratch, this book offers the tools, techniques, and strategies necessary to protect what matters most to your business.

New recruits crossing the Polish / Ukrainian border after training to defend their country © Bob Marshall 2004

INTRODUCTION

In today's world, security is far more than a set of static measures or a checklist of protocols. It is a dynamic and ever-evolving field that requires relentless vigilance, adaptability, and a forward-thinking mindset. Effective security is not just about putting up walls or nstalling digital firewalls; t is about cultivating a pervasive culture of security that influences every facet of your organisation.

This culture must be grounded in a robust and adaptable framework capable of addressing a broad spectrum of potential threats—ranging from financial crimes and data breaches to insider threats and physical intrusions.

In this book, you will discover how to carry out a comprehensive security footprint analysis—an essential process that allows you to identify your organisation's vulnerabilities and pinpoint areas for enhancement. This analysis is the foundation of any effective security strategy, enabling you to understand the full scope of risks and to develop targeted measures to mitigate them.

We will delve deeply into the various domains of security that are critical to protecting your organisation. You will learn about the pivotal roles of financial security in safeguarding assets and preventing fraud, information security in protecting sensitive data from cyber-attacks, human security in detecting and managing insider threats, technical security in leveraging technology to protect against both digital and physical risks, and physical security in defending against unauthorised access and environmental threats.

Beyond these foundational elements, this book will guide you through the complexities of managing security in diverse and often unpredictable environments. You will gain valuable insights into preparing for and responding to a range of security incidents, from minor breaches to full-scale crises. You'll also explore advanced strategies such as covert operations, intelligence gathering, and the use of surveillance to pre-empt and counteract threats.

We will cover how to build effective training programs that empower your staff to be vigilant and prepared, and how to create and implement contingency plans that ensure your organisation can swiftly recover from any disruption.

Throughout these chapters, you will learn that security is not a destination but a journey—a continuous process of evaluation, adaptation, and improvement. As you develop and refine your security strategy, you'll find that each step taken to strengthen your organisation's defences contributes to a safer, more resilient future.

Let us begin with the cornerstone of any effective security strategy:

The **Comprehensive Security Footprint Analysis**. This essential step will serve as your foundation, helping you to uncover potential risks and guiding you in crafting a strategy that is tailored to your organisation's unique needs and challenges.

Chapter One

Comprehensive Security Footprint Analysis

A comprehensive security footprint analysis is not a simple checklist or a routine audit; it is a thorough, systematic evaluation of every facet of your organisation's security profile. This deep-dive assessment goes beyond surface-level checks to uncover hidden vulnerabilities, assess potential threats, and design strategies tailored specifically to your organisation's needs. The goal is not only to identify gaps in existing defences but also to proactively anticipate and mitigate risks before they can materialise into real threats.

This analysis requires a holistic approach that examines and interconnects multiple security domains. It must account for financial, information, human, technical, and physical security. Each of these domains plays a vital role in protecting the organisation, and their integration is essential to creating a cohesive and adaptive security posture.

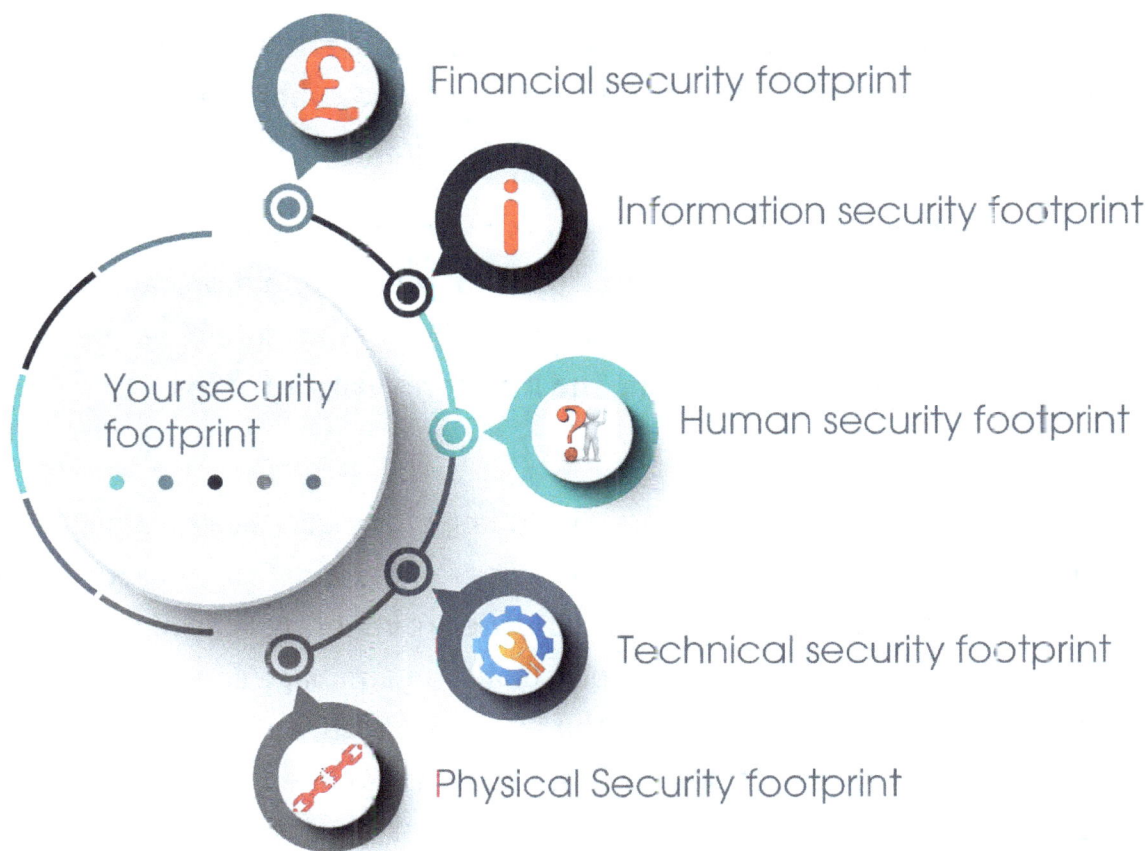

Financial Security

Protecting Your Organisation's Economic Assets from Multiple Threats

Financial security forms the backbone of an organisation's overall security strategy. It is crucial for safeguarding economic assets and resources from a wide array of threats, including fraud, embezzlement, cyber theft, money laundering, insider trading, and other financial crimes.

In today's complex and fast-paced business environment, the importance of financial security cannot be overstated. It is not merely about protecting money; it is about preserving the trust of stakeholders, maintaining operational continuity, and ensuring the long-term viability of the organisation.

Organisations across various sectors—including pharmaceuticals, retail, logistics, and transport—are particularly vulnerable to financial threats due to the nature of their operations. These industries routinely handle high-value transactions, maintain extensive supply chains, and manage sensitive financial information. In these environments, the stakes are high, and any breach in financial security can lead to severe consequences, including financial loss, reputational damage, regulatory penalties, and potential legal action. Thus, robust financial security protocols are not just recommended—they are essential for survival.

Understanding the Scope of Financial Security

Financial security encompasses a range of measures and controls designed to protect an organisation's economic resources. It involves safeguarding financial data, ensuring the integrity of financial transactions, and implementing mechanisms to prevent, detect, and respond to financial threats. These efforts must be comprehensive, encompassing every aspect of the organisation's financial operations and extending to all departments and personnel.

Preventing Fraud and Embezzlement

Fraud and embezzlement represent significant risks to financial security. These crimes can be committed by both internal and external actors, exploiting weaknesses in financial controls or taking advantage of inadequate oversight. Organisations must implement rigorous internal controls, such as segregation of duties, regular audits, and robust authorisation procedures, to prevent unauthorised access to financial resources. This includes deploying automated systems to detect irregularities, such as duplicate payments or unauthorised transactions, and conducting regular risk assessments to identify and address potential vulnerabilities.

Mitigating Cyber Theft and Digital Risks

With the increasing digitisation of financial processes, cyber theft has become one of the most prevalent threats to financial security. Hackers and cybercriminals target organisations' financial data through phishing attacks, ransomware, malware, and other sophisticated methods. Protecting against cyber theft requires a multi-layered approach that includes strong cybersecurity measures such as encryption, firewalls, secure authentication protocols, and continuous monitoring of financial networks for signs of unauthorised access or data breaches. Organisations must also ensure that employees are trained to recognise cyber threats and follow best practices for digital security.

Ensuring Compliance with Financial Regulations

Regulatory compliance is a critical component of financial security. Organisations must comply with a complex web of local, national, and international regulations governing financial transactions, reporting, anti-money laundering (AML) efforts, and anti-fraud measures. Non-compliance can result in severe penalties, including fines, sanctions, and legal consequences. To ensure compliance, organisations need to maintain accurate and transparent financial records, conduct regular internal audits, and stay up-to-date with changes in financial regulations and standards. Developing a strong compliance culture and providing regular training to employees on regulatory requirements are also essential.

Protecting Financial Data and Confidential Information

Financial data is one of the most valuable assets an organisation possesses. Protecting this data from unauthorised access, alteration, or destruction is critical to maintaining financial security. Organisations must implement robust data protection measures, such as encryption, access controls, secure data storage, and regular data backups. This also includes protecting sensitive information from insider threats, whether malicious or accidental, by implementing strict access controls, conducting regular audits, and fostering a culture of accountability and transparency. Some of this advice will be repeated within this book but it is essential to protect all aspects of financial security and data security.

Sector-Specific Financial Security Challenges

Each industry faces unique financial security challenges based on its specific operational and regulatory environment. Understanding these sector-specific threats is crucial for developing effective financial security strategies. In theory you can apply this understanding to any business sector.

Pharmaceutical Sector

The pharmaceutical industry is particularly vulnerable to financial risks due to its high-value products, complex supply chains, and stringent regulatory requirements. Financial security in this sector must address risks such as inventory theft, counterfeit drugs, billing discrepancies, and fraudulent claims. Organisations must implement robust financial controls, such as secure inventory management systems, supply chain verification processes, and automated billing and claims management tools, to protect against these threats.

Retail Sector

Retailers face unique financial security challenges related to point-of-sale (POS) systems, refund processes, and online payment gateways. Retail organisations must protect against risks such as skimming, credit card fraud, return fraud, and cyber-attacks. Financial security measures in this sector should include secure POS systems, encryption of payment data, real-time transaction monitoring, and strict controls over refund and return processes.

Logistics and Transport Sector

The logistics and transport sector is characterised by complex financial transactions involving multiple parties, international payments, and high-value cargo. Financial security must account for risks such as cargo theft, fraudulent billing, and financial losses due to delays or disruptions. Organisations should implement secure payment processing systems, conduct thorough due diligence on partners and suppliers, and use technologies such as blockchain to ensure the integrity of financial transactions.

General Considerations Across All Sectors

Regardless of the sector, certain financial security practices are universally applicable. These include maintaining accurate and transparent financial records, conducting regular risk assessments and audits, implementing internal controls and fraud detection mechanisms, ensuring compliance with financial regulations, and fostering a culture of vigilance and accountability.

Building a Robust Financial Security Framework

To effectively protect against financial threats, organisations must develop a comprehensive financial security framework that integrates multiple layers of defence.

This framework should include

Internal Controls and Audit Mechanisms

Establishing strong internal controls is essential for preventing unauthorised access to financial resources and detecting potential fraud or embezzlement. Regular audits, both internal and external, help ensure that financial processes are being followed correctly and that any discrepancies are quickly identified and addressed.

Advanced Fraud Detection and Prevention Technologies

Leveraging technologies such as artificial intelligence (AI) and machine learning (ML) can enhance the organisation's ability to detect and prevent financial threats. These tools can analyse vast amounts of financial data in real-time to identify anomalies, patterns, and trends that may indicate fraudulent activity.

Employee Training and Awareness Programs

Employees are often the first line of defence against financial threats. Regular training and awareness programs help employees recognise potential risks, understand the importance of financial security, and follow best practices for safeguarding financial assets. This includes training on recognising phishing attempts, secure handling of sensitive financial data, and reporting suspicious activities.

Incident Response and Recovery Planning

How we deal with an incident and how we recover is covered many times in this book for the simple reason that despite the best preventive measures, financial incidents can still occur. A comprehensive financial security strategy includes robust incident response and recovery plans that outline clear procedures for detecting, containing, and mitigating financial threats, as well as for recovering from incidents and restoring normal operations.

Continuous Monitoring and Improvement

Financial security is not a static goal but a dynamic process that requires continuous monitoring, evaluation, and improvement. Organisations must regularly review their financial security measures, update them in response to new threats, and ensure that they remain effective and aligned with industry best practices and regulatory requirements.

Financial Security as a Pillar of Organisational Resilience

Financial security is a critical component of an organisation's overall security strategy. By implementing a robust, multi-layered approach that encompasses prevention, detection, response, and compliance, organisations can protect their economic assets and resources from a wide range of financial threats. In an increasingly complex and interconnected world, maintaining strong financial security protocols is not just a matter of compliance—it is essential for the survival, growth, and long-term success of the organisation.

Information Security

Information security is dedicated to safeguarding an organisation's data against unauthorised access, data breaches, and a wide range of cyber threats. This involves developing and implementing a comprehensive strategy that includes multiple layers of protection.

First, data classification is essential to identify and categorise sensitve information based on its level of importance and the impact of potential exposure. This helps in determining the appropriate security measures for different types of data.

Access controls are another critical component, ensuring that only authorised personnel have access to specific data, systems, or networks. This involves using techniques such as multi-factor authentication, role-based access control, and regular monitoring of access logs.

Encryption plays a vital role in protecting data both in transit and at rest, by converting it into unreadable formats that can only be deciphered by those with the correct decryption keys. This ensures that even if data is intercepted or stolen, it remains inaccessible to unauthorised users.

Finally, incident response is a key part of an effective information security strategy. This involves preparing for, detecting, and responding to security incidents in a timely manner to minimise damage, recover quickly, and prevent future occurrences. It includes defining roles and responsibilities, establishing communication plans, and conducting regular drills to ensure readiness for potential cyberattacks.

By integrating these elements into a cohesive strategy, organisations can better protect their data assets from a constantly evolving threat landscape.

Data Classification and Governance

Start by establishing a robust data classification framework that categorises data based on its sensitivity, criticality, and the potential impact of exposure or loss. Typical categories might include "public," "internal," "confidential," and "restricted." Each classification should have clearly defined criteria and specific handling, storage, and protection requirements to ensure data is managed appropriately throughout its lifecycle.

For example, in the pharmaceutical industry, data categorised as "confidential" could include patient health records, proprietary drug formulas, clinical trial data, and other sensitive information. This type of data requires stringent protection measures, such as encryption both in transit and at rest, multi-factor authentication for access, and storage in secure environments with restricted physical and digital access. For "restricted" data, which may represent the highest level of sensitivity, additional safeguards like hardware security modules (HSMs), advanced intrusion detection systems (IDS), and frequent security audits should be implemented.

To effectively manage data across the organisation, develop comprehensive data governance policies. These policies should clearly define data ownership and assign specific roles and responsibilities for managing different types of data. This includes specifying who is authorised to create, modify, access, or delete data, and under what circumstances. Access controls should be enforced based on the principle of least privilege, ensuring that individuals only have access to the data necessary for their job functions.

Additionally, data governance policies should outline data retention and destruction requirements to ensure data is only kept for as long as needed for business or regulatory purposes. This involves implementing automated tools to monitor and enforce data retention schedules, securely deleting or anonymising data when it is no longer required, and documenting all data handling activities for auditing purposes.

Compliance with relevant regulations, such as the General Data Protection Regulation (GDPR) in the UK and European Union or the Health Insurance Portability and Accountability Act (HIPAA) in the United States, is critical. Ensure that your data governance policies are aligned with these legal requirements, which may dictate specific data protection measures, reporting obligations, and penalties for non-compliance. Regular audits and assessments should be conducted to verify compliance and identify areas for improvement in data management practices.

By implementing a structured approach to data classification and governance, organisations can protect their most valuable information assets, minimise risk, and ensure regulatory compliance in a complex and evolving data landscape.

Adopt Advanced Access Control Models

To effectively limit data access to authorised personnel, organisations should implement advanced access control models such as Role-Based Access Control (RBAC) and Attribute-Based Access Control (ABAC). These models provide a structured, scalable approach to managing access permissions, ensuring that users can only access the data necessary to perform their specific job functions while minimising the risk of unauthorised access or data breaches. Failure to comply with these simple guidelines has led to many large companies falling foul of unauthorised data breaches.

Role-Based Access Control (RBAC)

RBAC assigns access permissions based on an individual's role within the organisation. For example, in a logistics company, an employee in the warehouse might have access only to inventory management systems, while a customer service representative might have access to customer contact information but not too sensitive financial data. Access rights are predefined according to each role, reducing the risk of granting excessive privileges. This model simplifies administration by allowing access controls to be managed collectively at the role level rather than individually for each user, making it easier to implement and maintain consistent security policies across the organisation.

Attribute-Based Access Control (ABAC)

ABAC goes a step further by considering multiple attributes, such as user identity, job function, location, time of access, and data sensitivity level, to determine access rights. For instance, a retail manager might only be able to access sales data during business hours and only from a company device. This approach allows for more granular control, enabling dynamic decision-making based on real-time contextual factors. It is particularly beneficial in environments where access needs frequently change or depend on multiple criteria, such as multinational corporations with diverse teams and data access requirements.

Layered Access Control for Specific Sectors

In sectors like logistics, retail, or supply chain management, where multiple employees may require access to overlapping data sets—such as customer information, shipment tracking details, and supply chain analytics—adopt a layered access control approach. This involves creating different levels or layers of access permissions that correspond to distinct roles and responsibilities. For example:

Basic Level Access

Frontline employees, such as customer service agents, may be granted access to view customer orders and shipment statuses.

Intermediate Level Access

Managers might have permissions to modify customer information, approve refunds, or analyse sales data.

Advanced Level Access

Executives or data analysts may have access to aggregate data, business intelligence dashboards, and sensitive financial information for strategic decision-making.

Each layer is carefully defined to prevent unnecessary data exposure and ensure that each employee has the minimum necessary access for their job function.

Implement Strong Authentication Mechanisms

To further enhance security, especially for access to highly sensitive data, organisations should implement strong authentication mechanisms such as biometric verification and Multi-Factor Authentication (MFA). Biometric verification uses unique physical characteristics—like fingerprints, facial recognition, or iris scans—to verify identity, offering a high level of assurance that only authorized individuals can access sensitive data.

Multi-Factor Authentication (MFA) adds an additional layer of security by requiring users to provide two or more forms of verification, such as a password, a one-time code sent to a mobile device, or a hardware security token. This makes it significantly more difficult for attackers to gain unauthorised access, even if one authentication factor is compromised.

Continuous Monitoring and Auditing

As mentioned in the financial section of this book; to maintain the effectiveness of these access control measures, organisations should also implement continuous monitoring and auditing of access logs. Automated systems can detect and flag unusual access patterns or behaviours, such as attempts to access sensitive data outside of normal business hours or from an unusual location. Regular audits of access controls and permissions should be conducted to identify potential vulnerabilities, ensure compliance with internal policies and regulatory requirements, and make necessary adjustments.

By adopting advanced access control models like RBAC and ABAC, implementing strong authentication mechanisms, and employing continuous monitoring, organisations can significantly reduce the risk of unauthorised access, protect sensitive data, and maintain the integrity of their information systems.

Encryption and Data Loss Prevention (DLP)

Encryption is crucial for safeguarding data both in transit and at rest. Use strong encryption protocols such as AES-256 for all sensitive data. Implement Data Loss Prevention (DLP) tools to monitor and control data flows, preventing unauthorised access or accidental leaks. For example, in the transport industry, where data is often transmitted between different systems and locations,

DLP solutions can prevent sensitive data like route plans or cargo details from being intercepted or mishandled.

Incident Response and Recovery Planning

You will hear this mentioned several times in this book as it is essential to develop a robust incident response plan that includes clear protocols for detecting, responding to, and recovering from data breaches. This plan should detail the steps to contain a breach, assess the impact, notify stakeholders, and recover lost or compromised data.

Conduct regular tabletop exercises and simulations to test your organisation's preparedness and refine your response plans based on lessons learned.

Human Security

Protecting People as the Core Asset of Your Organisation

Human security focuses on safeguarding the most critical asset of any organisation: its people. This involves protecting employees, contractors, and visitors from internal and external threats, while creating secure environments that promote safety, trust, and productivity. Effective human security goes beyond physical measures—it includes fostering a culture of awareness, resilience, and preparedness, where every individual knows how to identify, respond to, and report potential risks.

Conducting Comprehensive Threat Assessments

Regular and comprehensive threat assessments are the foundation of human security. These assessments help organisations identify potential risks to personnel, including crime, workplace violence, political unrest, terrorism, and natural disasters. In environments where risk is inherently higher—such as conflict zones, politically unstable regions, or areas with high crime rates—these assessments should be conducted more frequently and adapted to evolving conditions.

High-Risk Environments

In regions like Ukraine, parts of the Middle East, or Central Africa, where political instability or armed conflict may pose a significant threat, organisations should increase the frequency of their threat assessments. For example, a non-governmental organisation (NGO) operating in a conflict zone may conduct weekly risk evaluations, using intelligence reports and local sources to identify potential threats such as planned attacks, protests, or hostile movements.

High Risk Environments – Irony of War, £250,000 Maybank travelling in one direction and an armoured personal tank traveling in the opposite direction – Polish / Ukraine Border © Bob Marshall

Advanced Risk Modelling

To better anticipate and prepare for various threats, organisations can utilise advanced risk modelling tools that analyse historical data, current events, and predictive algorithms to forecast the likelihood of different scenarios. For instance, a multinational corporation with operations in politically sensitive areas might use risk modelling software to predict the likelihood of civil unrest or terrorist attacks and adjust their security protocols accordingly.

Adaptive Mitigation Strategies

Based on the findings from threat assessments, organisations should develop adaptive mitigation strategies tailored to specific risks. For example, a business operating in a high-crime area could implement measures such as secure transportation for employees, staggered work shifts to reduce crowding at entry and exit points, and increased security personnel during high-risk periods.

Managing Insider Threats

Insider threats—those that originate from within the organisation, such as employees, contractors, or trusted partners—are among the most challenging to detect and mitigate. These threats can arise from various motivations, including financial gain, ideological beliefs, personal grievances, or even unintentional negligence. To effectively manage insider threats, organisations must implement proactive programs that monitor, detect, and respond to suspicious behaviour.

Monitoring and Behavioural Analytics

Utilise behavioural analytics tools to monitor for deviations from normal behaviour patterns that could indicate a potential insider threat. For example, a financial institution may employ software that detects unusual access patterns to sensitive data, such as an employee accessing large volumes of client information outside of their typical working hours. This can trigger an alert for further investigation.

Regular Background Checks

Conduct regular and thorough background checks on employees, contractors, and partners, not only at the time of hiring but periodically throughout their tenure. In sensitive sectors like finance, healthcare, or defence, background checks should be comprehensive, including criminal history, credit checks, and verification of qualifications. This helps to identify any changes in circumstances that could increase the risk of insider threats.

Training and Security Awareness

Regularly train employees to recognise and report signs of insider threats, such as colleagues displaying sudden changes in behaviour, violating security protocols, or accessing unauthorised areas. For example, in the IT sector, employees could be trained to spot signs of social engineering or phishing attempts that could compromise internal security. Creating a culture of security awareness and encouraging open communication can significantly reduce the risk of insider threats going undetected.

Designing Secure Work Environments

Creating a secure work environment involves integrating multiple layers of security measures to protect against both internal and external threats. These measures should include physical security, access controls, surveillance systems, and well-practiced emergency response plans. The design should be customised to the specific needs of the organisation, considering factors such as the type of business, location, and potential risks.

Layered Security in Physical Spaces

In a warehouse or logistics setting, where theft and unauthorized access are common concerns, organisations can implement multiple layers of security. For example: This is an overview, but we will go into more detail later in the book.

Surveillance Systems

Install CCTV cameras to monitor all entry points, loading docks, storage areas, and perimeter fences. Cameras should be connected to a central monitoring system that provides real-time alerts to security personnel.

Access Controls

Use biometric scanners or smart cards for access to sensitive areas, such as inventory storage or server rooms. This prevents unauthorised personnel from entering high-risk areas and creates an audit trail of who accessed these spaces and when.

Emergency Response Plans

Develop and regularly practice emergency response plans for various scenarios, such as fire, active shooter, or natural disaster. Conduct security drills to ensure all employees understand and can execute emergency protocols effectively.

Designing for Employee Safety

In high-risk environments, such as corporate offices in major cities or facilities located in areas prone to natural disasters, consider the layout and design of the workplace to enhance safety. This could include:

Safe Rooms or Shelters

Designate safe rooms equipped with emergency supplies, communication devices, and first aid kits in areas prone to natural disasters or civil unrest.

Controlled Access Points

Implement turnstiles, security checkpoints, or mantraps at key entry points to control access and prevent unauthorised entry.

Visibility and Lighting

Ensure that work areas, parking areas, and pathways are well-lit and free from obstructions, reducing the risk of crime or accidents.

Supporting Employee Well-Being and Resilience

A critical aspect of human security is supporting employee well-being and resilience. This is often overlooked. Employees who feel safe, supported, and valued are more likely to be productive, engaged, and vigilant against potential threats. Organisations should create programs and resources that help employees manage stress, cope with trauma, and build resilience against adversity.

Mental Health and Wellness Programs

Offer comprehensive mental health resources, such as access to counsellors, stress management workshops, and mental health days. For example, in industries like emergency response, healthcare, or transport, where employees face high levels of stress, specialised training in managing workplace stress and conflict resolution can be invaluable. This training could include mindfulness techniques, resilience-building exercises, and de-escalation tactics.

Employee Assistance Programs (EAPs)

Implement Employee Assistance Programs that provide confidential support for personal or work-related issues, including financial advice, psychological counselling, and legal assistance. For example, a logistics company could offer an EAP to help employees cope with the pressures of long hours, high-stress situations, or the impact of working in remote or hostile environments.

Open Communication Channels

Establish open communication channels that allow employees to report concerns or threats without fear of retaliation. For instance, a manufacturing company might set up an anonymous hotline or online reporting tool where employees can safely report suspicious activities, safety concerns, or workplace harassment. An open-door policy encourages employees to share information, which can be crucial in identifying and mitigating threats early on.

Resilience Training

Provide training that builds resilience against various threats. This could include crisis management training, self-defence classes, or training on how to recognise and respond to signs of mental distress in colleagues. In high-risk sectors, such as law enforcement or military, resilience training could be expanded to include psychological preparation for dealing with trauma and post-traumatic stress disorder (PTSD).

Building a Culture of Human Security

Human security is not just about protective measures—it's about fostering a culture where security is a shared responsibility. By conducting regular threat assessments, managing insider threats, designing secure environments, and supporting employee well-being, organisations can create a robust human security strategy that protects their most important asset—their people. In doing so, they build a resilient organisation where employees feel safe, empowered, and engaged in protecting both themselves and the organisation's broader interests.

Technical Security

Safeguarding Digital Assets and IT Infrastructure

Technical security is the cornerstone of an organisation's overall security posture, focused on protecting IT infrastructure, digital assets, and sensitive data from a range of cyber threats. This requires a comprehensive approach to securing networks, endpoints, data, and systems, while ensuring rapid response to incidents and evolving threats. The goal is not just to prevent breaches but to build a resilient environment that can withstand and recover from attacks.

Securing Networks and Endpoints

Protecting networks and endpoints is the first line of defence against cyber threats. A robust security framework should include a **defence-in-depth strategy** that employs multiple layers of security controls to protect against different types of attacks.

Firewalls and Intrusion Detection Systems (IDS)

Install and configure firewalls to filter and monitor incoming and outgoing traffic, blocking malicious activities. Complement this with IDS to detect and alert on any suspicious activities or potential breaches. For example, in the financial sector, firewalls can be set up to block traffic from regions known for cybercrime, while IDS can monitor for abnormal access patterns that suggest insider threats or compromised accounts.

Endpoint Protection and Regular Patching

Ensure all endpoints, including desktops, laptops, servers, and mobile devices, are protected with antivirus software, encryption, and regular patching to fix known vulnerabilities. In the logistics industry, where devices such as GPS trackers and mobile scanners are widely used, securing these endpoints is critical. For example, deploying **Mobile Device Management (MDM) tools** can enforce security policies such as strong passwords, remote wiping, and app restrictions to prevent unauthorised access.

Access Controls and Encryption

Implement strong access controls, including multi-factor authentication (MFA), to ensure that only authorised personnel can access sensitive systems. For organisations with remote or field-based employees, such as those in retail or logistics, encryption should be applied to all data transmitted over the network to protect it from interception or tampering.

Ensuring Data Integrity and Availability

Maintaining the integrity and availability of data is essential for business continuity and compliance. This involves protecting data from unauthorised access, tampering, and loss while ensuring it remains accessible to authorised users.

Data Integrity Measures

Use cryptographic methods like hashing and digital signatures to detect unauthorised changes to data. For example, in the healthcare sector, cryptographic hashes can be applied to patient records to ensure they remain unchanged from their original state. If data is altered, the hash value changes, indicating potential tampering.

Regular Backups and Redundancy

Regularly back up all critical data to mitigate the risk of data loss due to cyberattacks, hardware failure, or natural disasters. In sectors like retail and logistics, cloud-based storage solutions with automated backups provide an effective way to ensure data availability. For example, an e-commerce company might use a multi-region cloud backup strategy to ensure that customer data and order information are replicated across multiple geographic locations, ensuring continued access even in the event of a regional outage.

Disaster Recovery Plans

Develop and regularly test a comprehensive disaster recovery plan that outlines steps for restoring data and systems following a security incident. This plan should include predefined recovery point objectives (RPOs) and recovery time objectives (RTOs) to minimise downtime. For instance, a financial institution may have an RTO of two hours for critical transaction processing systems to ensure minimal disruption to its customers.

Conducting Regular Vulnerability Assessments

Vulnerability assessments are essential for identifying and addressing weaknesses in an organisation's IT infrastructure before they can be exploited by attackers. These assessments should be both automated and manual to simulate real-world attack scenarios.

Automated Tools and Manual Penetration Testing

Use automated vulnerability scanners to regularly assess the security of networks, servers, and applications. Complement this with manual penetration testing by ethical hackers who can identify complex vulnerabilities that automated tools might miss. For example, a financial services company could use automated tools to scan its online banking platform for known vulnerabilities, while ethical hackers attempt to find logic flaws or vulnerabilities in the application's business logic.

Third-Party Risk Assessments

Regularly assess third-party integrations for potential vulnerabilities. For example, in the supply chain sector, organisations should evaluate the security of partners' systems that have access to their network. A logistics company might audit the security practices of its transport partners to ensure they adhere to security standards that protect shared data.

Prioritised Remediation Plans

Develop a prioritised remediation plan that focuses on addressing the most critical vulnerabilities first. This might involve patching software, reconfiguring firewalls, or removing outdated protocols. For example, after a vulnerability assessment reveals that a critical application is using an outdated version of OpenSSL, the organisation's IT team should immediately apply the latest security patches.

Establishing Security Monitoring and Incident Response

Proactive monitoring and rapid incident response are crucial for minimizing the impact of security incidents. Organisations must be able to detect, analyse, and respond to threats in real time to prevent or mitigate damage.

Security Information and Event Management (SIEM) Systems

Deploy a SIEM system to collect and analyse security data from various sources, such as network devices, servers, and applications. This enables real-time threat detection and alerts. For example, an e-commerce platform might

use a SIEM to detect and respond to unusual spikes in login attempts, which could indicate a brute-force attack.

Incident Response Teams and Protocols

Establish a dedicated incident response team trained to handle various cyber incidents, from data breaches to ransomware attacks. Develop and regularly update incident response protocols that outline specific steps for containing, eradicating, and recovering from incidents. For instance, a bank may have a playbook that details the exact actions to take if a breach is detected, such as isolating affected systems, notifying stakeholders, and conducting forensic analysis.

Regular Drills and Updates

Conduct regular drills to test the effectiveness of incident response protocols. Simulate different types of attacks, such as phishing or DDoS attacks, to assess how quickly and effectively the organisation can respond. Based on the outcomes, update response plans to address any gaps or inefficiencies. For example, a healthcare organisation might simulate a ransomware attack to test its ability to quickly disconnect infected systems from the network and restore data from backups.

Building a Resilient Technical Security Framework

Technical security is an ongoing process that requires vigilance, adaptability, and continuous improvement. By securing networks and endpoints, ensuring data integrity and availability, conducting regular vulnerability assessments, and establishing robust monitoring and incident response capabilities, organisations can build a resilient technical security framework that protects against a wide range of cyber threats. The key is to remain proactive—anticipating threats before they materialise, responding swiftly to incidents, and continuously evolving security practices to stay ahead of attackers. In doing so, organisations not only protect their digital assets but also build trust and confidence with their customers, partners, and stakeholders.

Physical Security

Protecting Facilities, Assets, and Personnel from Physical Threats

Physical security is a critical aspect of an organisation's overall security strategy, focusing on the protection of facilities, assets, and personnel from a wide range of threats, including unauthorised access, theft, vandalism, and natural disasters. Effective physical security integrates well-designed environments, advanced access control, surveillance, and comprehensive emergency preparedness.

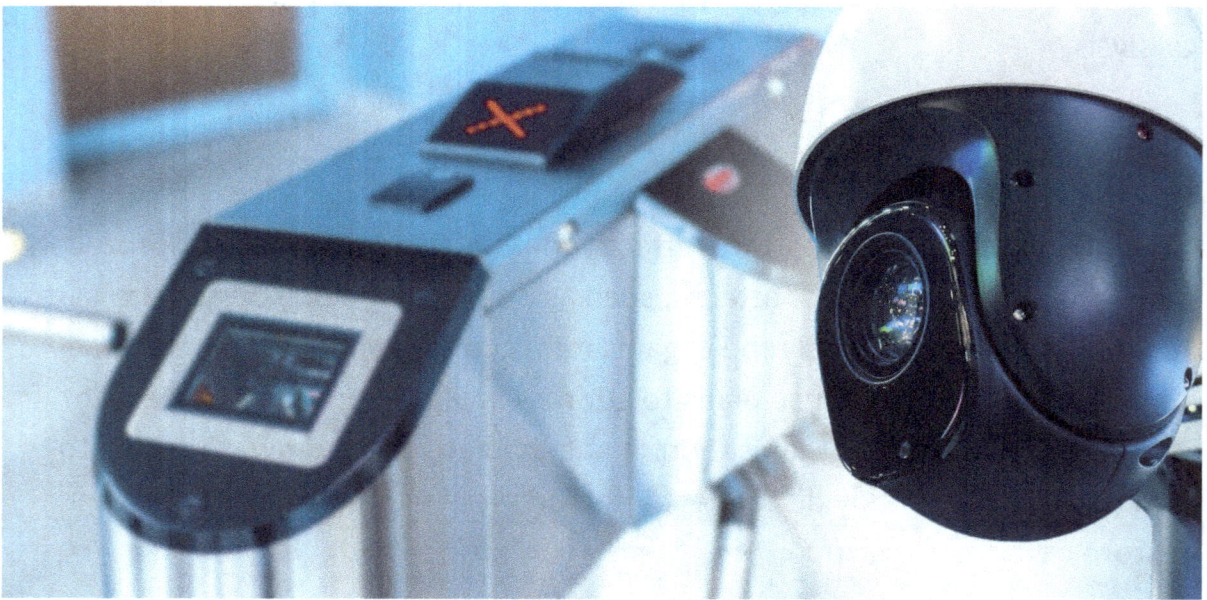

Implementing Secure Facility Design

The design of a facility plays a pivotal role in deterring and mitigating security threats. By applying **Crime Prevention Through Environmental Design (CPTED)** principles, organisations can create an environment that discourages criminal activity and enhances safety.

Applying CPTED Principles

Design facility layouts with clear sightlines, secure entry points, and minimal blind spots. Use natural surveillance techniques, such as strategic placement of windows and lighting, to increase visibility and deter intruders. For example, an office building might use landscaping to create clear paths and remove potential hiding spots around the perimeter.

Designating Secure Zones

In environments like warehouses, designate secure zones for high-value or sensitive items. Use additional barriers, such as secure cages or vaults, reinforced doors, and restricted access to these zones. For example, a pharmaceutical distribution centre may have a controlled-access area for narcotics, with biometric readers and CCTV cameras to monitor entry and exit.

Regular Facility Design Reviews

Regularly assess the facility design to ensure it meets current security needs. For instance, if a company expands its operations or introduces new high-value inventory, reassess the layout to determine if additional security measures are required.

Access Control Systems

Access control is a fundamental component of physical security, preventing unauthorised individuals from entering restricted areas. A robust access control system should be multi-layered, integrating various methods to ensure only authorised personnel gain access.

Layered Access Control

Implement a combination of access control methods, such as proximity cards, biometric readers, turnstiles, and security gates. For example, in a data centre, use biometric readers for access to server rooms, while requiring proximity cards for entry to the building.

Monitoring and Reviewing Access Logs

Ensure all access points are monitored around the clock with access control logs reviewed regularly for anomalies. For example, an anomaly might include an employee accessing a restricted area outside of their normal work hours. Investigate and address any discrepancies immediately.

Tiered Access Control for Complex Properties

In multi-tenant properties or facilities with high foot traffic, implement tiered access control where different levels of clearance are required for different areas. For example, a corporate office building could have a general access area for all employees, but restricted access zones for IT or executive offices that require additional security clearances.

Surveillance and Monitoring

Surveillance is a vital element of physical security, providing real-time monitoring and historical records to detect, deter, and respond to threats.

Comprehensive Surveillance Systems

Deploy a network of high-definition cameras, motion detectors, and automated alert systems to cover all critical areas. Integrate these with access control and alarm systems for a coordinated security response. For example, in a retail store, strategically place cameras at all entry and exit points, cash registers, storage areas, and blind spots to deter theft and monitor suspicious behaviour. Remember more fixed cameras are better then less moving cameras (PTZ).

Analytics and Real-Time Detection

Use video analytics software to detect and alert on unusual activities, such as loitering near secure zones, unauthorised access attempts, or tampering with merchandise. For example, in a bank, surveillance cameras with facial recognition could identify known offenders or alert security to suspicious behaviours like customers lingering near the vault or ATMs.

Remote Monitoring Capabilities

Integrate surveillance systems with remote monitoring solutions to allow security personnel to monitor facilities from a central location or through mobile devices. This is especially useful for organisations with multiple locations, such as retail chains or logistics companies, where security staff can monitor all sites simultaneously.

Emergency Preparedness

Emergency preparedness is essential to minimise harm and ensure a swift response to incidents such as natural disasters, fire, medical emergencies, or security threats. Comprehensive emergency plans should be regularly reviewed and practiced.

Developing Comprehensive Emergency Response Plans

Develop detailed emergency response plans that include procedures for various scenarios like evacuations, lockdowns, medical emergencies, and natural disasters. For example, a manufacturing plant should have a plan for hazardous material spills, including evacuation routes, spill containment procedures, and first-aid responses.

Specific Protocols for High-Risk Scenarios

In industries like logistics, establish protocols for securing vehicles and cargo during emergencies. Train drivers on alternative routes, secure parking areas, and communication protocols during incidents like civil unrest or natural disasters. For example, a trucking company operating in regions prone to hurricanes should have specific plans for rerouting deliveries, securing vehicles, and protecting cargo.

Regular Drills and Training

Conduct regular drills with all employees and stakeholders to test and refine emergency plans, ensuring that everyone understands their roles and responsibilities. For example, in a high-rise office building, conduct fire drills quarterly to practice evacuation routes, use of emergency exits, and coordination with local emergency services.

Integrating Technology with Emergency Plans

Utilise mass notification systems to quickly alert all employees of an emergency and provide instructions. Mobile apps or SMS alerts can be used to communicate with employees in real time, providing updates and ensuring safety. For example, a university campus could use a notification system to alert students and staff of an active shooter situation and provide instructions to shelter in place.

Building a Resilient Physical Security Framework

From my experience physical security is about more than just locks and cameras; it's about creating a layered defence strategy that integrates secure facility design, robust access control, comprehensive surveillance, and effective emergency preparedness. By adopting these practices, organisations can mitigate the risks associated with unauthorised access, theft, vandalism, and natural disasters, creating a safer environment for their personnel, assets, and operations.

To build a resilient physical security framework, organisations must regularly review and adapt their security measures to evolving threats, incorporate technological advancements, and maintain a culture of awareness and preparedness. This proactive approach not only protects physical assets but also instils confidence among employees, customers, and stakeholders that their safety and security are a top priority.

Chapter 2

Adaptive Security Environment Management

Crafting a Dynamic and Evolving Security Posture

Adaptive security environment management is an advanced approach to security that focuses on creating a dynamic and responsive security posture capable of evolving to meet emerging threats and challenges. This proactive strategy goes beyond static security measures by emphasising the need for continuous adaptation, foresight, and flexibility in addressing both current and anticipated security risks.

Covert Operations

Discreetly Identifying and Mitigating High-Risk Threats

Covert operations are a critical component of advanced security strategies, focusing on the discreet identification and mitigation of high-risk threats. These operations involve a range of tactics and techniques designed to operate under the radar, gathering intelligence and addressing security risks without alerting potential adversaries. Effective covert operations require meticulous planning, precise execution, and the ability to adapt to evolving situations.

Planning and Preparation Strategic Objective Setting

Before initiating any covert operation, clearly define the strategic objectives. Determine the specific threats to be addressed, such as internal sabotage, criminal infiltration, or corporate espionage. For instance, a tech company suspecting industrial espionage might set objectives to uncover how competitors are acquiring sensitive information and to identify the individuals involved.

Operational Planning and Resource Allocation

Develop a comprehensive operational plan that includes detailed procedures, roles, and resource requirements. This might involve designing surveillance setups, coordinating with undercover operatives, and acquiring necessary equipment. For example, in a covert operation to investigate potential insider threats, the plan might include deploying undercover security personnel, using hidden surveillance devices, and coordinating with human resources for potential interviews.

Intelligence Gathering & Undercover Surveillance

Conduct undercover surveillance to monitor suspected individuals or activities discreetly. This may involve physical surveillance, such as following individuals or observing locations, or digital surveillance, including monitoring email communications and network activities. For example, in a retail setting, undercover agents might observe employees to detect theft or fraudulent activities without alerting staff to the investigation.

Informant and Source Management

Utilise informants or confidential sources to gather intelligence from within the organisation or community. These sources provide valuable insights that are not accessible through conventional means. For instance, in a financial institution, an informant within the organisation could provide information on suspicious transactions or insider trading activities.

Execution of Covert Tactics & Discrete Interventions

Implement covert interventions to address identified threats without exposing the operation. This may include quietly removing compromised personnel, securing sensitive areas, or intercepting illicit activities. For example, if an investigation reveals unauthorised access to a secure facility, security teams might discreetly reinforce access controls and remove unauthorised individuals without publicising the breach.

Evidence Collection and Analysis

Collect and analyse evidence obtained during covert operations to support security measures or legal actions. This involves documenting findings in a manner that preserves the integrity of the evidence and ensures it is admissible in court if necessary. For example, in a corporate espionage case, detailed records of intercepted communications and surveillance footage may be compiled to support legal action against the perpetrators.

Post-Operation Review & Assessment and Reporting

After completing a covert operation, conduct a thorough assessment to evaluate its effectiveness and impact. Prepare detailed reports outlining the findings, actions taken, and any lessons learned. For example, following an undercover investigation into internal theft, a report might summarise the scope of the theft, identify weaknesses in existing security measures, and recommend improvements.

Adjustments and Follow-Up Actions

Based on the findings and assessment, implement any necessary changes to security protocols or operational procedures. Follow up on any unresolved issues or new threats identified during the operation. For instance, if an operation uncovers a pattern of theft linked to specific weaknesses in security policies, those policies should be revised and additional training provided to staff.

The Vital Role of Covert Operations in Comprehensive Security

Covert operations are essential for addressing high-risk threats with discretion and precision. By focusing on strategic planning, intelligence gathering, covert execution, and thorough post-operation review, organisations can effectively identify and mitigate risks that may not be visible through standard security measures.

The use of covert operations allows for a deeper understanding of potential threats, providing insights and evidence that inform more effective security strategies. Whether it involves investigating internal threats, detecting criminal activities, or gathering intelligence on competitive threats, covert operations enhance an organisation's ability to respond to and manage complex security challenges.

Ultimately, the successful execution of covert operations strengthens an organisation's overall security posture, ensuring a more robust defence against both known and emerging threats. Embracing these tactics fosters a proactive and comprehensive approach to security, helping organisations stay ahead of potential risks and safeguard their assets, personnel, and reputation.

Employ a combination of techniques, such as human intelligence (HUMINT), signals intelligence (SIGINT), and open-source intelligence (OSINT). HUMINT could involve working with local contacts or embedding agents within targeted organisations.

SIGINT might involve intercepting communications to understand threat actor plans, while OSINT can provide valuable insights from public sources, like social media or local news.

Ensure all intelligence activities comply with local and international laws and are ethically conducted.

Based on the intelligence gathered, implement measures to mitigate identified risks. This might include reinforcing physical security, changing operational procedures, or altering travel routes.

In regions with high levels of criminal activity or insurgency, such as parts of Africa or the Middle East, additional security measures could involve increasing patrols, enhancing surveillance, and deploying armed security personnel.

Regularly review and adjust covert operation strategies to ensure they remain effective and responsive to changing conditions.

Training and Development

Building a Well-Prepared Security Team

A well-trained team is the cornerstone of an effective security strategy. Comprehensive training and continuous development tailored to the specific needs of your organisation are essential for maintaining a robust security posture. This approach ensures that employees are not only aware of security protocols but are also prepared to respond effectively to various threats.

Comprehensive Training Programs & Designing Tailored Training Modules

When developing training programmes, it is essential to create a comprehensive approach that encompasses a wide range of security areas. These programmes should not be generic; instead, they must be specifically tailored to reflect the unique risks, challenges, and operational requirements of your organisation. Each organisation faces its own set of threats, from physical and digital security breaches to insider threats and regulatory compliance issues. Therefore, the training modules should be customised to address these specific concerns, ensuring that employees are well-equipped to recognise and respond to the particular threats they might encounter in their roles.

To achieve this, the training design process should begin with a thorough assessment of the organisation's risk landscape. This includes understanding the nature of the business, the environment in which it operates, and the specific vulnerabilities that are most likely to be exploited. From there, training modules can be developed to focus on areas such as cybersecurity best practices, data protection, physical security protocols, emergency response procedures, and awareness of social engineering tactics.

Additionally, the training should be adaptable and scalable, allowing it to evolve as new risks emerge or as the organisation's needs change over time. By continuously evaluating and refining the content, you ensure that your team is always prepared to handle the latest security challenges effectively. In this way, a well-designed training programme not only protects your organisation's assets but also fosters a culture of security awareness and resilience among employees.

Transport Industry Secure Cargo Handling

Provide comprehensive training for employees on best practices for securing cargo during transport. This training should cover the correct use of tamper-evident seals to prevent unauthorised access and manipulation, as well as secure loading techniques that minimise the risk of theft or damage. Employees should be taught how to identify potential security vulnerabilities in the cargo handling process and how to respond effectively to any threats.

The training should also emphasise the importance of maintaining a chain of custody, documenting all handling procedures, and regularly inspecting cargo for signs of tampering or damage. By ensuring that all staff members are well-versed in these practices, you can significantly reduce the risks associated with transporting valuable or sensitive goods, maintaining both the safety of the cargo and the reputation of your organisation.

Evasive Driving Techniques

Implement specialised driving courses that focus on teaching evasive manoeuvres and defensive driving strategies to prepare drivers for potential hijacking attempts and other security threats. These courses should cover a range of essential skills, including how to recognise and respond to suspicious vehicles or behaviours, execute sudden direction changes, accelerate or decelerate rapidly, and manoeuvre through tight spaces to evade attackers.

Additionally, the training should emphasise situational awareness, enabling drivers to anticipate potential threats before they materialise and make quick, informed decisions under pressure. Instructors should incorporate realistic scenarios and practical exercises that simulate high-risk situations, allowing drivers to practise their skills in a controlled environment. By equipping drivers with these advanced techniques, you can enhance their ability to protect themselves, their passengers, and their cargo in dangerous situations, thereby strengthening the overall security posture of your organisation.

Hijacking Protocols

Develop comprehensive procedures for effectively responding to hijacking situations, ensuring that all employees are well-prepared to handle such emergencies. These protocols should include clear communication guidelines to ensure that drivers, security personnel, and management can quickly and accurately report a hijacking incident. Establish secure channels for immediate contact with company headquarters, local law enforcement, and any relevant emergency response teams, ensuring that critical information is relayed without delay.

The protocols should also define specific roles and responsibilities for each team member during a hijacking, outlining steps for coordinating with law enforcement agencies and other authorities to secure the safety of personnel and assets. Procedures should cover a range of scenarios, including both on-road and off-road hijackings, with guidance on how to manage passenger safety, secure cargo, and de-escalate situations whenever possible.

Regular training and drills should be conducted to familiarise employees with these procedures and ensure they are confident in executing them under pressure. By establishing well-defined hijacking protocols, your organisation can minimise risks, respond swiftly and effectively to threats, and protect the safety and wellbeing of all involved.

Retail Sector Theft Prevention

Provide comprehensive training to employees on identifying and responding to potential theft-related threats. This training should focus on recognising suspicious behaviour, such as unusual movements, frequent loitering, or attempts to bypass security measures. Employees should be skilled in conducting security checks, such as verifying identification, inspecting packages, and monitoring access points to ensure that only authorised personnel are allowed entry.

Additionally, training should cover the effective use of loss prevention systems, including surveillance cameras, alarms, and inventory management tools. Employees should understand how to use these systems proactively to deter theft, as well as how to respond quickly and appropriately if a theft is detected. Regular refresher courses and scenario-based exercises can help ensure that all personnel remain vigilant and well-prepared to prevent and address potential theft incidents.

Conflict De-escalation

Equip employees with techniques for managing and de-escalating conflicts with customers or individuals displaying aggressive behaviour. Training should focus on developing strong communication skills, such as active listening, maintaining a calm tone, and using non-confrontational body language. Employees should learn how to assess the situation quickly, identify potential triggers, and apply de-escalation strategies, such as setting boundaries, offering solutions, or finding ways to reduce tension.

Role-playing exercises and simulations can be particularly effective in helping employees practice these techniques in a controlled environment, building confidence and ensuring they are prepared to handle real-life situations. By training staff to manage conflicts effectively, you not only reduce the risk of escalation and violence but also help to maintain a safe and positive environment for both employees and customers.

Active Shooter Response

Prepare employees to respond effectively in the event of an active shooter situation by providing specialised training on emergency procedures. This training should cover key response strategies, including the "Run, Hide, Fight" protocol: when to evacuate the premises, how to find secure hiding places, and, as a last resort, how to defend themselves if confronted by the attacker.

Employees should be familiar with lockdown procedures, such as securing doors, turning off lights, and silencing mobile devices, as well as the locations of safe rooms and designated evacuation routes. Regular drills should be conducted to ensure that employees understand their roles, can act quickly under pressure, and are aware of the best practices for communication with emergency services and law enforcement during a crisis.

By providing thorough training on how to respond during an active shooter situation, you enhance the safety and resilience of your workplace, equipping employees with the knowledge and skills needed to protect themselves and others in a life-threatening scenario.

Scenario-Based Training & Simulating Real-World Incidents
Cybersecurity Training & Simulated Cyber-Attacks

Implement regular cybersecurity training exercises that simulate real-world cyber threats, such as phishing attacks, malware infections, and data breaches. These exercises are designed to help employees recognise common attack vectors and respond effectively to potential cyber threats in real-time. Phishing simulations, for instance, can teach employees how to identify suspicious emails or messages, verify the authenticity of links and attachments, and report potential phishing attempts to the IT department. Simulations of malware infections or ransomware attacks can help employees understand the consequences of downloading malicious files or clicking on compromised links, while data breach scenarios can demonstrate the importance of securing sensitive information and following data protection protocols. By incorporating these hands-on exercises into your cybersecurity training programme, you not only raise awareness of potential threats but also foster a culture of vigilance and proactive defence. Regular simulations help employees stay alert to evolving cyber risks, practice appropriate responses, and build the confidence needed to mitigate threats effectively. This approach significantly reduces the likelihood of successful attacks, protecting both the organisation's digital assets and its reputation.

Incident Response Drills

Design and implement comprehensive incident response drills to prepare staff for effectively managing simulated data breaches. These exercises should provide a realistic scenario where participants must navigate the full range of incident response procedures, from initial detection through to resolution and reporting.

The drills should start with a simulated data breach scenario that reflects potential real-world incidents, such as unauthorised access to sensitive information or a ransomware attack. Staff should be required to identify the signs of a breach, such as unusual system activity or unexplained data changes, and take immediate action to contain the incident.

Key elements of the drill should include:

Isolation of Affected Systems

Staff must practice the process of isolating compromised systems to prevent further damage or data loss. This involves disconnecting affected devices from the network, restricting access, and ensuring that no additional data is transmitted or altered.

Incident Reporting

Employees should be trained on the proper channels and protocols for reporting a breach. This includes notifying the IT department and management promptly, providing detailed information about the incident, and documenting all actions taken during the response.

Coordination and Communication

The drill should emphasise the importance of internal coordination and communication. Staff should work collaboratively with IT and management to assess the impact of the breach, determine the necessary remedial actions, and ensure that all relevant stakeholders are kept informed.

Post-Incident Review

After the drill, conduct a thorough review of the response to identify strengths and areas for improvement. This includes analysing the effectiveness of the isolation procedures, the accuracy of the incident reports, and the efficiency of internal communications. Use these insights to refine the incident response plan and enhance preparedness for future scenarios.

By regularly conducting detailed incident response drills, you ensure that your staff are well-prepared to manage real data breaches effectively. These exercises not only improve their ability to handle security incidents but also strengthen the overall incident response capabilities of your organisation, helping to mitigate potential risks and minimise damage.

Pharmaceutical Sector Example

Contamination Incidents

Develop and conduct detailed simulations for scenarios involving the contamination of controlled substances to ensure employees are well-prepared to handle such critical situations effectively. These exercises should mimic realistic incidents where controlled substances—such as hazardous chemicals, biological agents, or pharmaceuticals—become inadvertently or intentionally contaminated, requiring immediate and appropriate response measures.

Key elements of these simulations should include:

Containment Procedures

Train employees on the specific procedures required to contain a contamination incident. This includes identifying and isolating the affected area to prevent the spread of the contaminant. Employees should practice using appropriate containment equipment, such as spill kits, protective barriers, and containment booms. Emphasise the importance of following established protocols for securing and handling contaminated materials to minimise exposure and environmental impact.

Reporting Procedures

Ensure that employees are familiar with the correct reporting channels and protocols for contamination incidents. This involves notifying the relevant internal teams, such as health and safety, facilities management, and senior management, as well as external authorities if required. Training should cover the precise information to be included in incident reports, such as the nature of the contamination, the location, potential impact, and actions taken.

Remediation Processes

Guide employees through the steps necessary for the safe and effective remediation of contamination incidents. This includes procedures for decontaminating affected areas, disposing of hazardous materials according to regulations, and conducting thorough clean-ups. Employees should understand how to implement corrective actions to address the source of contamination and prevent future occurrences.

Health and Safety Measures: Incorporate training on personal protective equipment (PPE) and safety measures to protect employees from exposure during a contamination incident. This includes correct usage of PPE, emergency decontamination procedures, and first aid measures for potential exposure.

Post-Incident Review

Following each simulation, conduct a comprehensive review to evaluate the effectiveness of the response and identify areas for improvement. Analyse the adherence to containment and reporting protocols, the efficiency of the remediation efforts, and the overall coordination among teams. Use feedback from these reviews to update and refine the incident response procedures, ensuring continuous improvement and enhanced preparedness.

By implementing detailed simulations for contamination incidents, you equip employees with the knowledge and skills needed to handle such emergencies effectively. These exercises help to ensure a swift, coordinated, and safe response, thereby protecting both personnel and the environment while maintaining compliance with relevant regulations.

Break-In Attempts

Organise and execute drills that simulate break-ins or theft attempts to enhance the preparedness of your staff and security teams. These drills should recreate realistic scenarios involving unauthorised entry or theft attempts, allowing employees to practice and refine their response procedures and coordination efforts.

Key components of these drills should include:

Simulated Break-In Scenarios

Design drills that mimic various break-in methods, such as forced entry, tampering with locks, or bypassing security systems. These simulations should be as realistic as possible to provide a true-to-life experience. The scenarios could include different times of day, varying levels of security, and diverse entry points to challenge employees and security teams.

Response Procedures

Train employees and security personnel on the correct procedures for responding to break-in attempts. This includes recognising signs of a breach, alerting the appropriate security teams or law enforcement, and initiating emergency protocols. Employees should practise locking down the premises, evacuating the area if necessary, and using any security measures in place, such as alarms or lockdown systems.

Coordination with Security Teams

Emphasise the importance of seamless communication and coordination with security teams during a break-in attempt. This includes establishing clear lines of communication, providing timely updates on the situation, and following instructions from security personnel or emergency responders. Drills should involve joint exercises where employees work in tandem with security teams to manage the situation effectively.

Assessment and Evaluation

After each drill, conduct a thorough debrief to assess the effectiveness of the response. Review the execution of response procedures, the effectiveness of coordination between employees and security teams, and the overall handling of the simulated incident. Identify strengths and areas for improvement and use this feedback to refine response protocols and enhance future training.

Post-Incident Review and Feedback

Analyse the drill results to understand what went well and what could be improved. Gather feedback from all participants to identify any gaps in procedures, communication issues, or areas where additional training might be needed. Implement changes based on these insights to improve overall readiness for actual break-in attempts.

By regularly conducting detailed break-in attempt drills, you ensure that employees and security teams are well-prepared to handle real security breaches effectively. These exercises not only enhance the security posture of your organisation but also foster a proactive and responsive culture among staff and security personnel.

Logistics Industry Example

Hijacking Drills

Conduct rigorous hijacking drills tailored to the logistics industry to assess the readiness and effectiveness of drivers and security personnel in responding to high-risk scenarios. These simulations should mirror realistic hijacking situations, involving potential threats to both vehicles and cargo.

Key elements of the drills include:

Simulated Hijacking Scenarios

Create various scenarios that reflect potential hijacking attempts, such as forced vehicle stops, confrontations with armed individuals, or attempts to commandeer the vehicle. Ensure these simulations account for different environments and conditions, such as remote locations or urban settings, to test adaptability.

Communication Protocols

Evaluate the effectiveness of communication protocols during a hijacking. This involves practising how drivers and security teams report the incident to the control centre or law enforcement, including the use of secure communication channels and timely information sharing.

Emergency Response

Train participants on emergency response procedures, including how to follow protocols for handling a hijacking, such as complying with demands when necessary, safeguarding cargo, and managing the safety of any passengers. Emphasise the importance of remaining calm and making decisions that minimise risk.

Effectiveness of Security Measures

Assess the implementation of security measures, such as vehicle tracking systems, alarm systems, and emergency alert mechanisms. Evaluate how well these measures support the response to a hijacking and identify any areas where improvements are needed.

Debrief and Analysis

After each drill, conduct a comprehensive debrief to analyse the response performance. Review the effectiveness of communication, the adequacy of emergency procedures, and the overall management of the simulated hijacking. Use insights from these evaluations to refine protocols and enhance training.

Theft Response

Implement targeted drills to practice and improve responses to theft incidents within the logistics sector. These exercises should focus on securing the area, reporting the theft, and conducting thorough investigations.

Key components of these drills include:

Simulated Theft Scenarios

Design drills that simulate different types of theft, such as cargo theft during transit, pilferage at storage facilities, or internal theft by staff. These scenarios should reflect realistic conditions and challenges faced in the logistics industry.

Securing the Area

Train staff on how to effectively secure the scene of a theft. This includes procedures for cordoning off the affected area to preserve evidence, preventing unauthorised access, and ensuring that no additional items are removed or tampered with.

Reporting Procedures

Practice the correct process for reporting theft incidents, including notifying the appropriate internal teams, such as security and management, as well as external authorities if required. Ensure that reports include detailed descriptions of the theft, the suspects if known, and the steps taken during the response.

Conducting Investigations

Equip employees with the skills to conduct initial investigations into theft incidents. This involves collecting and documenting evidence, such as surveillance footage, witness statements, and any physical evidence found at the scene. Train staff on how to work with law enforcement or private investigators to support the investigation.

Post-Incident Review

After each theft response drill, conduct a detailed review to evaluate the effectiveness of the response. Assess how well the area was secured, the timeliness and accuracy of the incident reporting, and the thoroughness of the investigation. Use feedback to improve procedures and enhance future training.

By regularly conducting these detailed drills, you ensure that drivers, security personnel, and other staff in the logistics industry are well-prepared to handle hijacking and theft incidents effectively. These exercises not only improve the security and safety of operations but also contribute to a proactive and responsive organisational culture.

Enhancing Security Through Continuous Training

Training and development are vital for ensuring that security teams are well-prepared to handle a range of threats effectively. By designing comprehensive training programs, employing scenario-based exercises, and conducting regular drills, organisations can equip their personnel with the knowledge and skills necessary to respond to security incidents with confidence.

This proactive approach to training helps to identify gaps in security measures, improve team performance, and enhance overall preparedness. Continuous development ensures that employees remain aware of the latest security threats and best practices, fostering a culture of vigilance and resilience within the organisation.

Ultimately, investing in thorough and ongoing training strengthens the organisation's security framework, ensuring that all personnel are ready to tackle emerging challenges and protect valuable assets effectively.

Contingency Planning

Preparing for the Unexpected

A security contingency plan is a critical component for businesses to ensure resilience against potential threats, including natural disasters, cyber-attacks, theft, and supply chain disruptions. For sectors like pharmaceuticals, retail, and logistics, the nature of risks and the strategies to mitigate them may differ. This report outlines a structured approach to creating a security contingency plan tailored to these industries, including identifying risks, designing response strategies, implementing safeguards, and continuously monitoring and revising the plan.

Risk Assessment and Analysis

Identify Potential Threats. Every business must start by identifying potential internal and external threats. For each industry:

Pharmaceuticals Industry Risks

Key threats include counterfeiting, supply chain disruptions, regulatory compliance failures, cyber-attacks targeting sensitive data, and insider threats.

Retail Industry Risks

Potential risks encompass theft (both customer and employee), data breaches (such as credit card fraud), supply chain disruptions, and natural disasters impacting physical stores or warehouses.

Logistical Industry Risks

Common threats include cargo theft, cyber-attacks targeting logistics software, transportation accidents, regulatory compliance issues, and natural disasters affecting supply chains.

Conduct a Vulnerability Assessment

Once threats are identified, assess the vulnerabilities within the business. Analyse existing security measures, both physical (such as locks, surveillance cameras, and guards) and digital (firewalls, encryption, access controls). Evaluate operational processes, such as inventory management in retail, cold chain management in pharmaceuticals, and route planning in logistics, to identify potential weak points. Assess the workforce's awareness and preparedness for security incidents.

Determine the Impact and Probability of Each Threat

For each identified threat, estimate the potential impact (financial loss, reputational damage, legal consequences) and the likelihood of occurrence. Use a risk matrix to prioritise threats based on their severity and probability.

Developing the Security Contingency Plan

Define Objectives and Scope

Clearly outline the objectives of the security contingency plan, such as safeguarding assets, ensuring the safety of personnel, maintaining regulatory compliance, and minimising operational downtime. Define the scope of the plan, specifying which assets, departments, and processes are covered.

Create Response Strategies

Develop specific strategies for responding to each identified threat. This includes:

Pharmaceutical Industry Response Strategy Example

Develop procedures for detecting and responding to counterfeit drugs, such as implementing blockchain-based tracking systems. Establish protocols for handling data breaches, including notifying affected parties and regulatory bodies.

Retail Industry Response Strategy Example

Create a plan for responding to theft, including collaboration with local law enforcement and use of anti-theft technologies like RFID tags and smart cameras. Establish a data breach response plan, including steps for securing customer data and public communication strategies.

Logistics Industry Response Strategy Example

Develop procedures for managing cargo theft, such as GPS tracking and collaboration with law enforcement agencies. Create response plans for natural disasters that affect transportation routes or warehouse operations, including rerouting strategies and contingency partnerships with alternate suppliers.

Implementation of Safeguards and Controls

Implement physical and digital security measures, deploy security controls based on the identified risks.

Pharmaceutical Industry Safeguards and Controls Example

Use secure storage facilities for sensitive products, implement access controls for restricted areas, and deploy robust cybersecurity measures to protect patient data and intellectual property.

Retail Industry Safeguards and Controls Example

Install surveillance systems, alarms, and electronic article surveillance (EAS) systems to prevent theft. Use strong encryption for payment processing and regularly update cybersecurity protocols.

Logistics Industry Safeguards and Controls Example

Use GPS tracking for fleet management, invest in secure transportation vehicles, employ automated security systems at warehouses, and enhance digital protections for logistics management systems.

Develop Training and Awareness Programmes

Train employees regularly on security procedures and contingency protocols. Conduct regular drills and simulations for various scenarios (e.g., fire drills, data breach simulations). Provide specific training sessions tailored to different departments and roles. Keep employees updated on the latest security threats and best practices.

Implement Redundancy and Backup Systems

Ensure that critical systems have redundancy and backups to minimise downtime, for example regularly back up data and ensure that backups are stored securely offsite. Establish alternative supply chains or suppliers in case of disruptions. For pharmaceuticals, consider redundant storage options to maintain cold chain integrity.

Monitoring, Testing, and Continuous Improvement

Conduct regular audits and assessments, regularly review the effectiveness of the security contingency plan, perform security audits to identify new vulnerabilities. Update risk assessments based on emerging threats or changes in the business environment.

Test the Plan Through Simulations

Run regular simulations to test the readiness of the plan and the response teams, conduct tabletop exercises for management to test decision-making processes. Carry out full-scale drills to evaluate the effectiveness of communication protocols, response strategies, and incident management.

Gather Feedback and Revise the Plan

After each test or actual incident, gather feedback from all stakeholders and revise the plan, accordingly, identify what worked well and where improvements are needed. Update procedures, roles, and responsibilities as required. Monitor and respond to emerging threats and stay informed about new and evolving threats. Subscribe to industry publications, attend security conferences, and engage with cybersecurity communities to stay up to date on the latest risks and best practices. Adjust the security contingency plan based on new threat intelligence.

Creating a robust security contingency plan is essential for businesses in sectors like pharmaceuticals, retail, and logistics. By systematically assessing risks, developing targeted response strategies, implementing appropriate safeguards, and continuously monitoring and updating the plan, businesses can effectively mitigate threats, ensure continuity, and protect their assets, personnel, and reputation.

I recommend creating a risk matrix template and an Incident response checklist and Communication Protocol Template.

By following this structured approach, businesses can build resilience against various threats, ensuring that they are well-prepared to respond swiftly and effectively in any emergency.

Command and Control

Coordinating Security Responses and Managing Critical Incidents

A robust command and control framework is crucial for managing and responding to security incidents effectively. This framework provides the structure needed to ensure that responses are well-coordinated, decisions are made quickly and accurately, and communication flows smoothly and securely across all levels of the organisation. To achieve this, it is essential to clearly define roles and responsibilities, establish reliable communication protocols, and implement decision-making processes that enable rapid and efficient management of critical incidents.

Defining Roles and Responsibilities

Incident Commander

The central authority responsible for overseeing the incident response, making strategic decisions, and ensuring that all actions are aligned with the organisation's objectives. The Incident Commander coordinates the efforts of all response teams and serves as the main point of contact for external parties, such as law enforcement and regulatory bodies.

Operational Response Team

This team is tasked with executing the tactical elements of the incident response plan. Their responsibilities may include securing the physical site, mitigating cyber threats, or managing supply chain disruptions. Members are assigned based on their expertise in relevant areas, such as IT, logistics, or facility management.

Communications Lead

Responsible for managing all internal and external communications during an incident. This role includes disseminating information to employees, stakeholders, customers, and the public, ensuring that messages are consistent, accurate, and timely.

Support Teams

These may include human resources, legal, and compliance teams that provide critical support, ensuring that all actions comply with legal requirements and internal policies, while also assisting with employee welfare and managing the post-incident review process.

Establishing Communication Protocols

Internal Communication Channels

Create clear, dedicated channels for internal communication during a critical incident. This could include secure messaging apps, internal email groups, and dedicated phone lines. It is essential to establish protocols that outline how information is shared, who is authorised to communicate, and how updates are provided to different teams.

External Communication Plans

Develop procedures for communicating with external stakeholders, such as customers, suppliers, law enforcement, and the media. Pre-drafted templates and designated spokespersons can help ensure consistency and speed in messaging. Protocols should also address how to handle sensitive information and manage public relations to mitigate reputational damage.

Communication Hierarchy and Frequency

Define a hierarchy of communication to ensure that critical information flows in a structured manner. Determine the frequency of updates, who needs to be informed at each stage, and how information should be escalated or de-escalated based on the incident's severity.

Implementing Decision-Making Frameworks

Incident Response Playbooks: Develop playbooks for different types of incidents (e.g., cyber-attacks, natural disasters, theft) that provide predefined decision-making frameworks. These playbooks should include step-by-step procedures, decision trees, and escalation paths to guide responders in real-time.

Rapid Decision-Making Models

Employ rapid decision-making models, such as the OODA Loop (Observe, Orient, Decide, Act) or Decision-Making Under Pressure (DMP) frameworks. These models help teams make swift and informed decisions based on the available data, the situation's urgency, and the potential impact of various actions.

Crisis Command Centre

Establish a physical or virtual command centre to serve as the central hub for coordinating the incident response. The command centre should be equipped with the necessary tools and technologies to monitor the situation, communicate with internal and external parties, and make real-time decisions.

Ensuring Flexibility and Scalability

Ensure that the command and control framework is flexible and can adapt to different types and scales of incidents. This may involve scaling up response efforts for major incidents or activating specific components of the framework for minor incidents.

Continuous Training and Drills

Conduct regular training sessions and simulations to familiarise all personnel with their roles and responsibilities within the command and control framework. Simulations should cover various scenarios to test the flexibility and responsiveness of the framework.

Feedback and Continuous Improvement

After each incident or drill, gather feedback from all involved parties to identify strengths and areas for improvement. Use this feedback to refine roles, communication protocols, and decision-making processes, ensuring that the framework remains effective and responsive to evolving threats.

An effective command and control framework is the cornerstone of a well-coordinated security response. By clearly defining roles and responsibilities, establishing robust communication protocols, and implementing structured decision-making processes, businesses can respond to critical incidents swiftly and efficiently, minimising damage and ensuring continuity. Regular training, continuous improvement, and adaptability are essential to maintaining a resilient and responsive security posture.

Virtual Security Footprint in a Business Security Environment

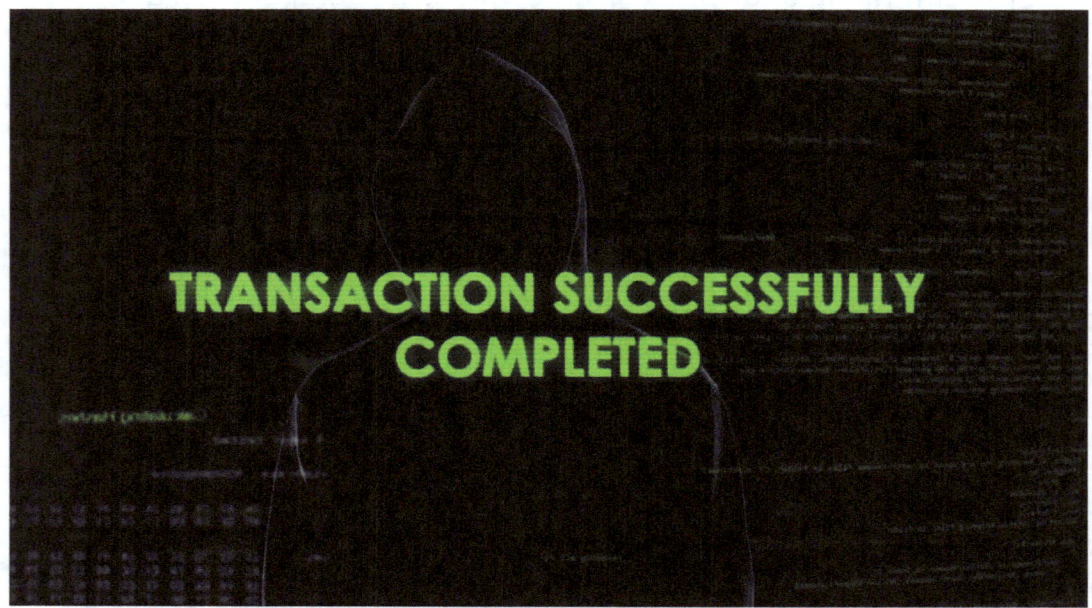

Some of this section I have covered earlier in this book, I make no apology for that, at the time of writing we are facing one of the most challenging times online, several wars, several countries highly active in the field of digital interference and every business should protect themselves.

According to various cybersecurity reports, there are approximately 2,200 cyber-attacks per day globally, which translates to about one attack every 39 seconds. Certain industries are targeted more frequently. Financial institutions can face upwards of 300,000 cyber-attacks per day, due to the high value of the data they hold. The healthcare sector is a major target, with some estimates indicating up to 1 million attacks per day against healthcare systems and providers globally. Retail businesses, particularly those with significant online presences, can see thousands of attacks daily, especially during peak shopping periods.

A virtual security footprint in a business security environment represents the entirety of an organisation's digital presence, including all digital assets, networks, data, and processes that must be protected from cyber threats. It is a comprehensive view of everything that constitutes a company's online and digital existence, outlining where potential vulnerabilities exist and how they are safeguarded. This footprint helps in establishing a clear picture of the digital attack surface, ensuring that all components of the digital environment are adequately protected.

Key Components of a Virtual Security Footprint

Data and Databases

This includes all proprietary information, such as customer data, financial records, trade secrets, intellectual property, employee information, and operational data. Databases, data lakes, and data warehouses must be secured through encryption, access controls, and regular backups.

Applications and Software

All business-critical software, including on-premises and cloud-based applications like CRM, ERP, HR management systems, and proprietary applications, form part of the virtual footprint. Protection measures include regular patching, secure coding practices, and application firewalls.

Websites and Online Portals

Company websites, customer-facing portals, and internal intranet sites are essential parts of the footprint. Web application firewalls (WAFs), secure socket layers (SSL/TLS), and regular security audits help protect these assets from threats such as SQL injection, cross-site scripting, and other vulnerabilities.

Internal Network

The internal network infrastructure, including Local Area Networks (LANs), routers, switches, and internal servers. Security measures involve segmentation (to isolate sensitive areas), intrusion detection and prevention systems (IDPS), and robust access controls to limit user privileges.

External Network Connections

Wide Area Networks (WANs), Virtual Private Networks (VPNs), and any other external connections to the internet or third-party networks. Security controls for these elements include encrypted communications, secure tunnelling protocols, and continuous monitoring for suspicious activities.

Endpoints

All devices that connect to the network, such as computers, mobile devices, tablets, printers, and Internet of Things (IoT) devices. Endpoints are protected using endpoint detection and response (EDR) tools, antivirus software, mobile device management (MDM) solutions, and strict patch management policies.

Cloud Infrastructure and Services

Many businesses use cloud environments for data storage, computing, and application hosting. The virtual footprint extends to all cloud-based services (such as AWS, Azure, or Google Cloud) and Software as a Service (SaaS) applications. Key security measures include identity and access management (IAM), secure configurations, encryption, regular vulnerability scanning, and compliance monitoring.

Third-Party Integrations

Connections with third-party service providers, APIs, and vendors integrated with the business's cloud environment. Security measures involve regularly assessing third-party risk, monitoring data flows, and ensuring third parties comply with the business's security standards.

Cybersecurity Measures

Firewalls and Gateways

Both hardware and software firewalls that protect the perimeter of the business's network, filtering traffic and blocking unauthorised access. Secure gateways provide additional protection by monitoring traffic between different network segments.

Identity and Access Management (IAM)

Systems that manage user identities and control access to critical assets and information. IAM solutions enforce strong password policies, multifactor authentication (MFA), and privileged access management (PAM) to ensure that only authorised users can access sensitive data.

Encryption

Encryption protocols protect data both at rest (stored data) and in transit (data moving across networks). End-to-end encryption, secure key management, and encryption for cloud storage are essential for safeguarding sensitive information.

Operational Security Protocols

Security Monitoring and Incident Detection

Continuous monitoring of network traffic, system logs, user behaviour, and application activities using Security Information and Event Management (SIEM) systems, Endpoint Detection and Response (EDR) tools, and Managed Detection and Response (MDR) services.

Incident Response Plan

A predefined set of actions to detect, respond to, and recover from security incidents. This plan includes the roles and responsibilities of the incident response team, steps for containment, mitigation, and recovery, and communication protocols with internal stakeholders and external entities.

Vulnerability Management

Regular vulnerability assessments and penetration testing to identify and remediate weaknesses in the system. This includes patch management, configuration reviews, and security audits to ensure that all systems are up-to-date and properly configured.

Compliance and Regulatory Controls

Compliance with Legal and Regulatory Standards

As I mentioned earlier adherence to data protection laws is paramount (such as GDPR, CCPA, HIPAA) and industry-specific regulations (like PCI-DSS for payment processing or ISO 27001 for information security management). This involves implementing technical and organisational measures to protect data and ensure legal compliance.

Data Governance Frameworks

Establishing clear policies and procedures for data management, retention, and disposal, aligned with regulatory requirements and best practices. This includes data classification, access controls, and regular audits to ensure compliance.

User Awareness and Training

Security Awareness Programmes

Regular training and awareness sessions to educate employees on cybersecurity threats, such as phishing, social engineering, and insider threats. Employees should also be trained on the proper use of business systems, secure password practices, and recognising potential security incidents.

Simulated Phishing Campaigns and Drills

Regularly conducting simulated phishing attacks and security drills to test employees' awareness and response capabilities, identifying areas that need further training or reinforcement.

Threat Intelligence Gathering

Using threat intelligence feeds and services to stay informed about emerging threats, vulnerabilities, and threat actors targeting the business or its industry. This allows for proactive adjustments to security measures and rapid response to new threats.

Behavioural Analytics

Implementing tools that use machine learning and artificial intelligence to analyse network traffic and user behaviour for anomalies that may indicate malicious activities.

Conclusion

Building a Resilient and Secure Organisation

By exploring the intricate aspects of security detailed throughout this book, you are now well-prepared to tackle the complex task of safeguarding your organisation. I have reiterated many aspects of the same theology in most of the subjects within my book, but to be successful in protecting your company understanding and implementing comprehensive security strategies will empower you to effectively assess risks, des gn robust measures, and stay adaptable to evolving threats.

Embracing Security as an Ongoing Process

Security is not merely a one-time objective but an ongoing journey that demands constant vigilance, flexibility, and refinement. As threats continue to evolve and new challenges emerge, your security posture must adapt to stay ahead. The principles and techniques outlined in this book provide a framework for maintaining a dynamic and resilient security environment.

Equipped for Comprehensive Security Management

The guidance provided here offers practical tools and insights to conduct thorough security analyses, implement effective countermeasures, and safeguard your organisation from diverse threats. Whether it's strengthening financial security, enhancing human safety, securing technical infrastructures, or developing contingency plans, the strategies detailed in this book are designed to address every facet of organisational security.

Key Takeaways:

Risk Assessment and Adaptation:

Learn to identify and evaluate potential risks through detailed assessments. Adapt your security strategies to address specific vulnerabilities and evolving threats effectively.

Implementation of Effective Measures:

Utilise the frameworks and solutions provided to implement robust security measures tailored to your organisation's needs. From physical security enhancements to technical safeguards, apply these measures to build a comprehensive defence.

Fostering a Culture of Security:

Promote a culture of safety and resilience within your organisation. Engage employees at all levels in security practices, encourage vigilance, and create an environment of trust and preparedness.

Preparing for Future Challenges

By embedding the principles and strategies discussed in this book into your security practices, you will strengthen your organisation's ability to face future challenges confidently. The commitment to continuous improvement and adaptation will ensure that your security measures remain effective in a rapidly changing threat landscape.

In conclusion, a strong security posture is not only about implementing the right tools and procedures but also about fostering a proactive and resilient mindset. With the knowledge gained from this book, you are equipped to build a more secure, resilient organisation ready to navigate any challenges that lie ahead.

About the Author

With over four decades of comprehensive experience in the security industry, I have dedicated my career to ensuring the safety and protection of organisations and individuals across a diverse range of global environments. My journey within the security domain has encompassed multiple sectors, each presenting distinct and evolving challenges. From the high-value pharmaceutical industry, where safeguarding sensitive assets and intellectual property is paramount, to the fast-paced retail environment, where theft prevention and crowd control are critical concerns, my expertise spans an array of demanding fields.

I have worked extensively in the transport and logistics sectors, where maintaining the integrity of supply chains and mitigating threats posed by both internal and external actors is vital to operational success. My involvement in property management has included developing robust security protocols for residential, commercial, and industrial sites, ensuring safety and security amidst complex urban challenges. Additionally, I have addressed the unique needs of warehousing and storage facilities, where safeguarding inventory from theft, damage, and unauthorised access requires specialised solutions.

My career has taken me far beyond the borders of the United Kingdom, immersing me in some of the most dynamic and high-risk regions of the world. From the war-torn landscapes of Ukraine, where conflict and instability create heightened security risks, to the rapidly developing and security-conscious environment of Dubai, I have navigated a broad spectrum of security challenges.

My work in France and Germany has involved adapting to regulatory frameworks and cultural nuances, while my experience in the USA has required an understanding of both federal and state-level security standards. Each location has deepened my understanding of the global security landscape and the importance of tailored, region-specific approaches.

This book is the culmination of a lifetime of dedication to the field of security. Drawing on my extensive global experience, it provides you with practical, actionable insights designed to strengthen your organisation's security posture. Whether you are protecting critical assets, managing risks in complex environments, or building resilience against emerging threats, the strategies within this book will equip you with the knowledge and tools necessary to safeguard what matters most.

Thank You for Reading

I sincerely appreciate the time and attention you've dedicated to reading this book. Security is a complex and ever-evolving field, and I hope that the insights, strategies, and practical advice shared throughout these pages serve as a valuable resource in your efforts to enhance your organisation's security infrastructure. Whether you are a seasoned professional looking to refine your approach or a leader seeking to establish a strong foundation in security protocols, my goal has been to provide actionable solutions that you can implement immediately to safeguard your assets, people, and operations.

In today's rapidly changing world, staying ahead of potential threats is more important than ever. The knowledge you've gained from this book is just one part of an ongoing journey towards building a resilient organisation. I encourage you to remain vigilant, continuously assess your security posture, and adapt to new challenges as they arise. The strategies outlined here are designed to be flexible and scalable, allowing you to customise them according to your organisation's unique needs and risk profile.

Should you have any further questions, require clarification on any of the topics discussed, or seek tailored advice specific to your situation, please do not hesitate to reach out. I am more than happy to offer additional guidance and support. You can easily contact me via my website at rmarsall.co.uk, where I provide a range of services, including personalised consultations, in-depth security assessments, and bespoke training programs aimed at addressing the challenges your organisation may face.

Your commitment to improving security is not only a testament to your dedication as a professional, but also a vital step in ensuring the long-term safety and success of your organisation. It is a responsibility that demands ongoing attention, and I am here to assist you every step of the way. Whether you are facing specific challenges or seeking to future-proof your organisation against emerging threats, I am available to offer the expertise and guidance necessary to achieve your security goals. Thank you once again for entrusting me with your time and attention. I look forward to supporting you on your path to a more secure and resilient future.

info@rmarshall.co.uk

https://rmarshall.co.uk

© 2004 V1 September 2004